THAT NEW BABY

This paperback edition published in 1984.

Published simultaneously in Canada by John
Wiley & Sons Canada, Limited, Rexdale, Ontario.

ISBN: 0-8027-7227-7

Library of Congress Catalog Card Number: 73-15271

Printed in the United States of America.

10   9   8   7   6   5   4   3   2   1

THAT NEW BABY

An Open Family Book For Parents And Children Together

by Sara Bonnett Stein

in cooperation with
Gilbert W. Kliman, M.D.
Director

Doris Ronald
Educational Director,
The Cornerstone Nursery-Kindergarten

Ann S. Kliman
Director,
Situational Crisis Service

Phyllis Schwartz
Community Coordinator

The Center for Preventive
Psychiatry
White Plains, New York

photography by Dick Frank
graphic design, Michel Goldberg

Walker and Company
New York, New York
Created by Media Projects Incorporated

A Note About This Book

When your child was a baby, you took him to the doctor to have him immunized for childhood illnesses. The injections hurt a little, but you knew they would prepare his body to cope with far more serious threats in the future. Yet there are other threats as painful and destructive to a child's growth as physical illness: Separation from his parents, a death in the family, a new baby, fears and fantasies of his own imagining that hurt as much as pain itself. These Open Family Books are to help adults prepare children for common hurts of childhood.

Caring adults try to protect their child from difficult events. But still that child has ears that overhear, eyes that read the faces of adults around him. If people are sad, he knows it. If people are worried, he knows it. If people are angry, he knows that too.

What he doesn't know—if no one tells him—is the whole story. In his attempts to make sense of what is going on around him, he fills in the fragments he has noticed with fantasied explanations of his own which, because he is a child, are often more frightening than the truth.

We protect children because we know them to be different, more easily damaged than ourselves. But the difference we sense is not widely understood. Children are more easily damaged because they cannot make distinctions yet between what is real and what is unreal, what is magic and what is logic. The tiger under a child's bed at night is as real to him as the tiger in the zoo. When he wishes a bad thing, he believes his wish can make the bad thing happen. His fearful imagining about what is going on grips him because he has no way to test the truth of it.

It is the job of parents to support and explain reality, to guide a child toward the truth even if it is painful. The dose may be small, just as a dose of vaccine is adjusted to the smallness of a baby; but even if it is a little at a time, it is only straightforwardness that gives children the internal strength to deal with things not as they imagine them to be but as they are.

To do that, parents need to understand what sorts of fears, fantasies, misunderstandings are common to early childhood—what they might expect at three years old, or at five or seven. They need simpler ways to explain the way

nplicated things are. The adult text of each of these
oks, in the left hand column, explains extraordinary
ys that ordinary children between three and eight years
attempt to make sense of difficult events in their lives.
uts in words uncomplicated ways to say things. It is
obably best to read the adult text several times before
a read the book to your child, so you will get a comfort-
e feel for the ideas and so you won't be distracted as you
k together. If your child can read, he may one day
curious to read the adult text. That's all right. What's
itten there is the same as what you are talking about
gether. The pictures and the words in large print are to
rt the talking between you and your child. The stories
intense enough to arouse curiosity and feeling. But they
reasonable, forthright and gentle, so a child can deal
th the material at whatever level he is ready for.

e themes in these Open Family Books are common to
ildren's play. That is no accident. Play, joyous but also
rious, is the way a child enacts himself a little bit at a
ne, to get used to events, thoughts and feelings he is
nfused about. Helping a child keep clear on the difference
tween what is real and what is fantasy will not restrict
hild's creativity in play. It will let him use fantasy more
ely because it is less frightening.

some ways, these books won't work. No matter how a
rent explains things, a child will misunderstand some
rt of the explanation, sometimes right away, sometimes
retrospect, weeks or even months later. Parents really
n't help this fact of psychological life. Nothing in human
owing works all at once, completely or forever. But
rents can keep the channels of communication open so
at gradually their growing child can bring his version of
e way things are closer to the reality. Each time you
ad an Open Family Book and talk about it together, your
ild will take in what at that moment is most useful to
m. Another day, another month, years later, other aspects
the book will be useful to him in quite different ways.
e book will not have changed; what he needs, what he
otices, how he uses it will change.

ut that is what these books are for: To open between adult
d child the potential for growth that exists in human
eings of all ages.

It is the special job of mothers and fathers to bring into life a new human being who reflects their form in his own perfect fingers, who has dignity in his solemn gaze, who speaks to them already in a language they have never learned and always known. It is also the special job of mothers and fathers to raise that baby, to lead and to follow their child into the path of his life. Birth is momentous; but raising children is continual. With a first baby, parents await the moment of his birth. With a second baby, parents await the moment and at the same time have a lot to see to in the everyday raising of the child they already have. Already there is no lap for Charles. And that's not all. Charles' crib will be the baby's. His highchair will be the baby's. His very baby clothes will be for someone new. To Charles, as to all children, it seems that a new baby replaces the old one. And why would a mother want a new baby, unless the old one were not good enough? That is the starting point: Jealousy begins before the new baby is born.

Before the new baby was born, there was already no lap for Charles.

So sometimes a child shares with gentle hands the unborn baby's kicking, and sometimes he "accidentally" bumps against his mother's belly, and sometimes openly, angrily, lunges into it. The special job of children is to make of those good feelings and those difficult feelings a way to master, a way to grow. You can help: Admire your child. He has grown big. He can do many things. You are glad you have him around to keep you company.

Give him the story of his own babyhood. What it was like inside you, and how he was born. That he was so small, and couldn't do much then. How you fed him his warm milk, and bathed his body, and smoothed his skin with powder. That you carried him, that you rocked him to sleep. That he got all the care that every baby needs.

To each child, the story of his own beginning tells who he is, where he came from, to whom he belongs. He need never, because he has the story, give up his babyhood entirely.

Parents can't guess everything that is on a child's mind. Melissa would so much like to have a baby of her own. She is confused and thinks that eating crackers is what makes a baby grow. She hopes they will make a baby grow in her too. It is her secret. No one knows she thinks that. Charles has wishes too: Like many other little boys, he plays at being pregnant. When Charles was born, Melissa was disappointed about something else: Charles was a boy. If Mommy and Daddy could make him with a penis, it seemed unfair that they should have made her without one.

These ideas make the roots of jealousy unique in each child. They grip him. They are difficult to unravel. The things Charles and Melissa wish and fear are common. A mother's pregnancy, a baby's birth, stimulate concerns and questions about a child's own body. It is a good time to speak plainly about sex and body parts. Little by little, a girl will understand that no one decided which sex she would be, and that she must wait until she grows up to have a baby. Little by little, a boy will understand his part in making babies too.

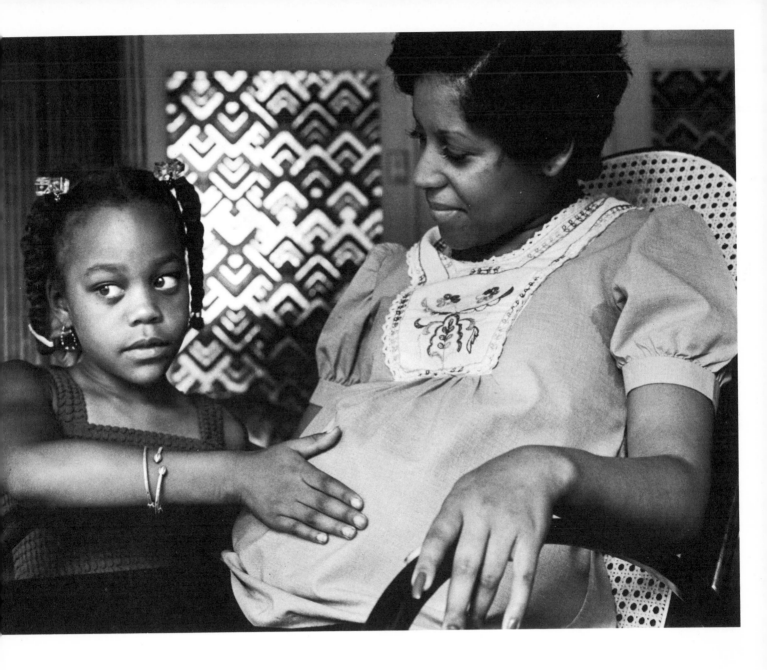

The baby in there was kicking.
Melissa could feel it.

Melissa ate crackers. She hoped they would make a baby in her.

Charles put
a pillow
under his
shirt so his
tummy
would look
big.

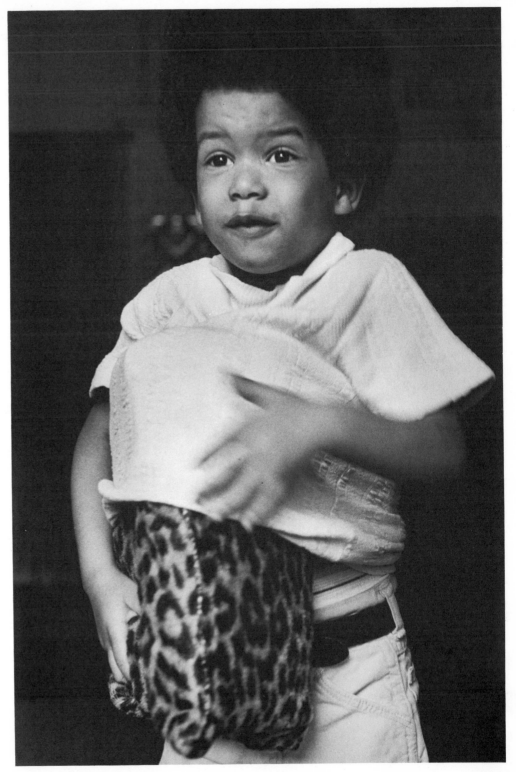

The baby's coming! But what seems to parents the bright beginning of a new life may seem to their child the end of their concern for his. His mother, his father, look worried to him. They rush and go away. They are leaving him behind.

Some things make it harder. It is hard to be taken off to a home he does not know. It is scary to be left with strangers. A child is stronger in his own home, with his father or grandmother or a babysitter he has known for a long time. A child feels better with what's old and comfortable and everyday—the same meals, baths, bed; the TV shows; the outdoor times and indoor times that have always held his day together. But what's ideal isn't always possible. If you can't leave your child at home with someone he knows, this is the second choice: A different home, but with someone he trusts, who will bring him back to Mommy. And the third choice: Someone he doesn't know, but in his own home, where Mommy will find him again.

The last choice, a stranger in a strange place, is a choice no parent should ever elect. It can be very scary for a little child.

One day Mommy felt the new baby wanting to be born. Grandma was there. Daddy took Mommy away to the hospital. The children hadn't even had dinner yet,

it was such a hurry.

Different mothers find different ways to keep a kind of contact with their child while they are gone. One mother and her children chose what would be good to eat and stocked the freezer with four favorite dinners. Another wrote a note in case she had to leave while her son was sleeping, as a way of kissing him good morning. Some mothers ask a child to water their favorite plant for them, or wind their alarm clock, or mark off on the calendar the few days they will be gone. It is a good idea, if your child is not used to talking to you on the telephone, to call him a few times during the weeks before you leave, so he will know your voice when you call from the hospital.

Show your child the hospital where you will be staying. Look in the gift shop. What might be a nice treat to bring home for him? Go to the desk and ask if this hospital has a brochure that describes their maternity services, so your child and you can see pictures of your room, and where the newborn babies sleep. Show him that there are telephones in a hospital, and write the number very big on a piece of paper. He can help you to tape it up on the wall at home.

A letter to read, a meal to eat, a job to do, a place he's seen, the voice he knows are ways to stay a little with a child even when you must be gone.

The next morning, Daddy said, "You have a new brother. Isn't that wonderful? He gave Charles a truck and Melissa a big baby doll.

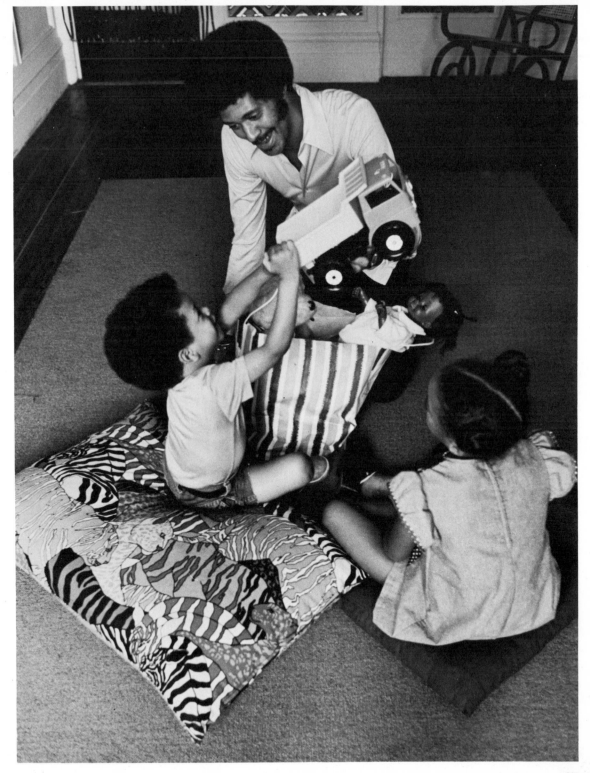

It is a beautiful, awkward, fragile moment: The new baby comes home to meet his family. A mother is excited, and still unsure; a father is pleased, and still not used to it. And a child has been waiting, almost forever, for the mommy he loves, for the baby he has never seen.

The moment is so high that it topples easily. Few children have seen a newborn baby. They expect something better. They should be warned: A new baby doesn't know anyone yet. He won't recognize his own family. He won't smile at them. He won't play with them.

Maybe Daddy could hold the baby. Maybe Grandma could put the baby in bed. What your child needs now is you. He could be angry: You have walked out on him. He could be whiney: He hopes he is still your baby. He could be demanding: It is his turn now.

Today Mommy comes home with the new baby.
He has a name.
His name is Darrell.

It is hard for a young child to make sense of what is going on. Why does Grandma love a baby that messes his pants? She scolds Charles if he does that. No one fusses much over baby spit up, baby drool; they fuss a lot about Charles' dirty face, Charles' runny nose. The baby cries and cries and cries. Charles isn't supposed to do that. It can help your child if you try to see the baby through his eyes, and agree with how things look: "I don't like it either when he drools on me." "He doesn't smell so good right now." "I wish he would stop crying and go to sleep." After all, your baby will not be insulted yet. And your child can afford generosity if he is allowed superiority.

"Isn't he precious," says Grandma.

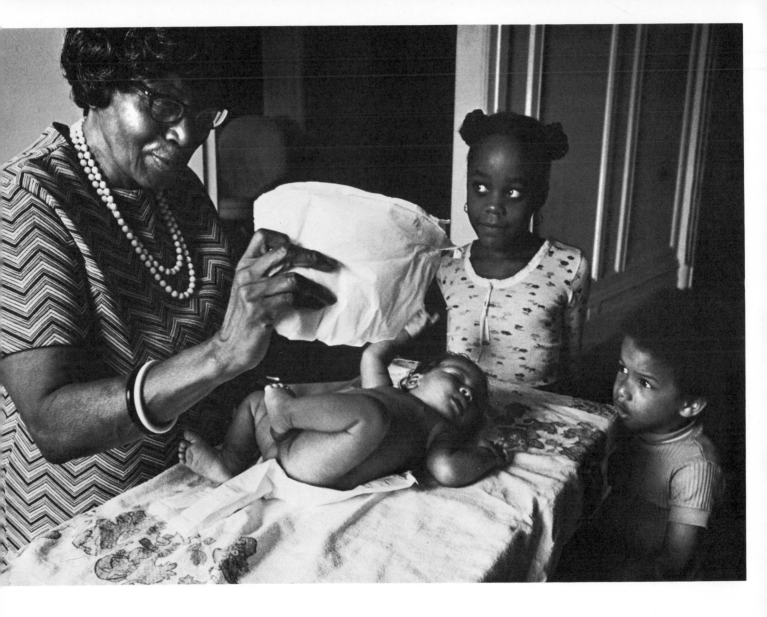

Here come the relatives. Here come the neighbors. Some, not meaning to, will spell trouble. People have a way of acting as though children are capable of only injury towards a new baby: Waking him, hurting him, making him cry, giving him germs. They have a way of touching sore spots. They say, "You don't really want your brother, do you? Shall I take him home with me?" And they have a way of bringing presents only for the baby, noticing only the baby, talking only about the baby. Of course a child is angry. Of course he blames that new baby.

It is up to you to stand up for the facts, to protect the feelings. The facts are that a baby sleeps perfectly well in a noisy home, that he does not break easily, and that everyone in a family shares the germs in the air they breathe. As to the feelings, point out to your child the presents people gave to celebrate his birth—the music box from Uncle Joe, the bunny from Mrs. Smith, the sweater Grandma knitted. When people tease or say silly things, you can try to stop them.

Everybody comes to see Darrell. Some of them say, "Shhhh, you'll wake him up." Some of them say, "Oh, don't touch him; you'll hurt him."

Maybe someone has said to Charles: "Won't it be fun to have a new brother or sister to play with?" But he won't be able to play with Darrell yet. Maybe someone has said to Melissa: "Are you going to take care of your new baby?" But there is little that Melissa can contribute now. A baby can be a disappointment to your child. And your child can be a disappointment to himself.

Things work out better if you explain more about what a baby can do, and what a child can do with him. How when a baby's cheek is touched, he will turn his head in that direction. How when the sole of his foot is stroked, he will curl his toes. And how if he is hungry, he will suck even on a hand or arm that happens to touch his mouth. If you are watching, your child can make the baby smell delicious with powder on his tummy; and make him burp, holding him across his lap. Let your child hold a shiny pie plate up for the baby to gaze at, or jingle a bunch of keys so the baby can find it with his eyes. Let him put a finger in the baby's hand and feel the tiny fingers grab tight on his.

But Charles and Melissa can do things with the baby, and do them very well.

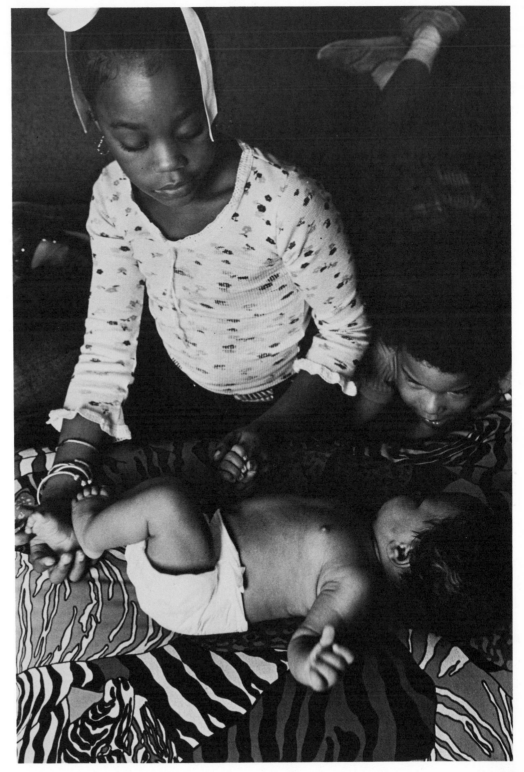

Being allowed to touch and hold and do things with a baby allows a child also to express the mixed-up jealous ways he feels. Charles calls his brother "it," as though he were not human. He carries him awkwardly; he won't make him comfortable. He rocks him too vigorously.

A mother and father can understand how a child feels: "I see you don't like babies very much today." But a mother and father must make a clear difference between the feelings they understand, and the actions they will allow: Darrell is not an "it;" he is a baby boy. No one is allowed to hurt him, or to be rough with him, or to make him uncomfortable.

Parents who can gently and firmly stop a child from actually hurting anyone show that they are strong enough to be the controls he does not yet have inside himself. He need not worry—they take care of him, and of the baby too. Charles' mother helps another way: "You could rock a baby doll," she says.

"It wants to go to bed" says Charles. He rocks Darrell too hard. His Mommy stops him. No one is allowed to hurt a baby.

When Charles plays, it is another way of helping himself express the way he feels just then. He wishes that the baby would smash up. Or be lost. Or one day simply disappear. The playing can't hurt Darrell.

He plays some games by himself. He gives the baby doll a ride in his truck. She keeps falling out. His Mommy says, "I see you don't like babies very much today."

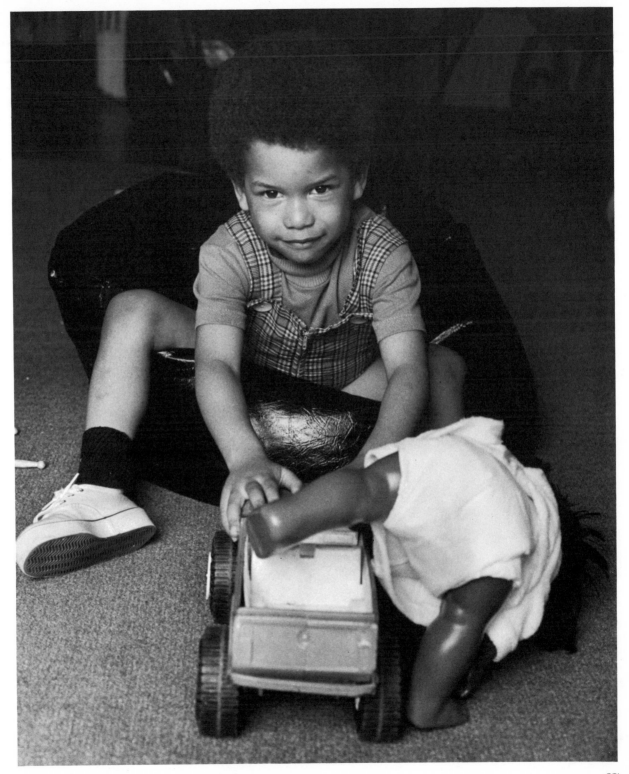

But like all children under eight, Charles believes that wishing makes things happen. He is not sure where the boundary is between what he thinks about and how things really are. He thinks mean thoughts against the baby and then gets scared of what his thoughts might do to him. He may feel that he is bad. He may fear that he is dangerous. When parents let a child say his wishes or pretend them or play them out, it shows they can handle such things. Perhaps what a child says makes them uncomfortable, perhaps they really don't like it at all. But they do not believe in its power to do real harm.

Charles' mother, when she says, "We can throw bugs away, but never babies," is clearly reassuring him about the difference between make-believe and real.

He finds little balls o fluff on the rug.
He pretends
they are babies.
"Baby bug, baby bug,
fly away," he sings.
His mother says,
"We can throw
bugs away,
but never babies."

29

Charles tries but can't go back again. He will never fit into baby clothes again. He will never be rocked in his carriage. Another child might so long to go back to a time when less was asked of him, when he felt more secure, that he may start again to wet his pants or bed, to need a bottle. Maybe he will act silly, talk baby talk, cry a lot, cling to you wherever you go. He feels pretty sure he is good at being a baby. He is not so sure he is good at being a big boy. When you look at these pictures, sympathize together with your child about Charles—how nice it must seem to him to be a baby again, cuddled and cared for, having his mommy all to himself.

There is an old game a child and his mother can play together: "You be the mommy; I'll be your baby." Pretending like this is another kind of boundary that parents help their children build. It puts the urge to go backwards outside the frame of what is real—it is "only pretend." And within a frame of time—you only play it for a little while.

Charles is too big for Darrell's clothes. And too big for his carriage too. But he pretends he is his Mommy's baby bird, so she will feed him.

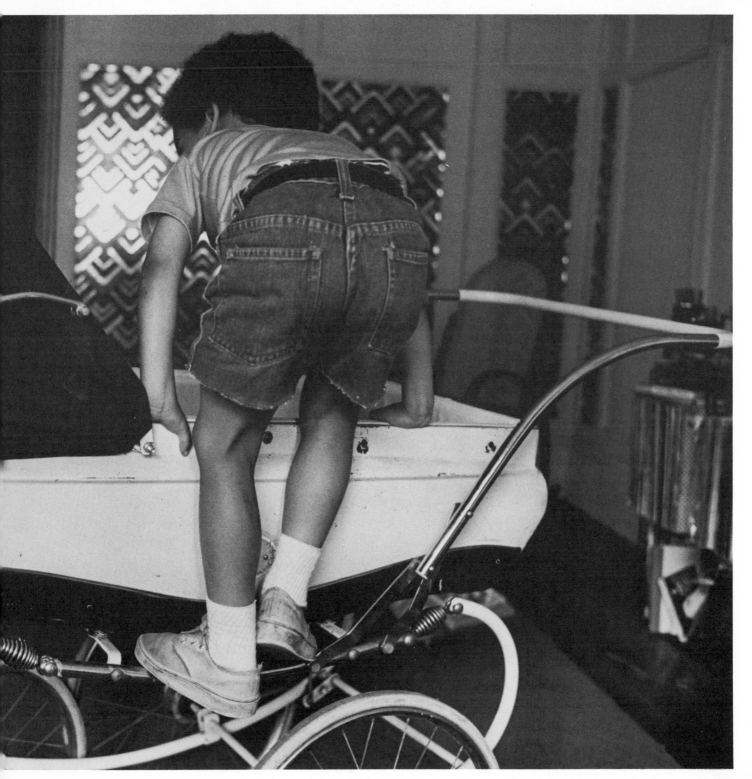

Just as Charles has had to face the fact that he is too old to be a baby, Melissa has to face the fact that she is too young to have a baby. Daddy and Mommy have a real baby; they only gave Melissa a doll.

Melissa's baby doll is too small to wear the real baby's clothes. The real baby keeps on growing. But Melissa's baby doll doesn't grow.

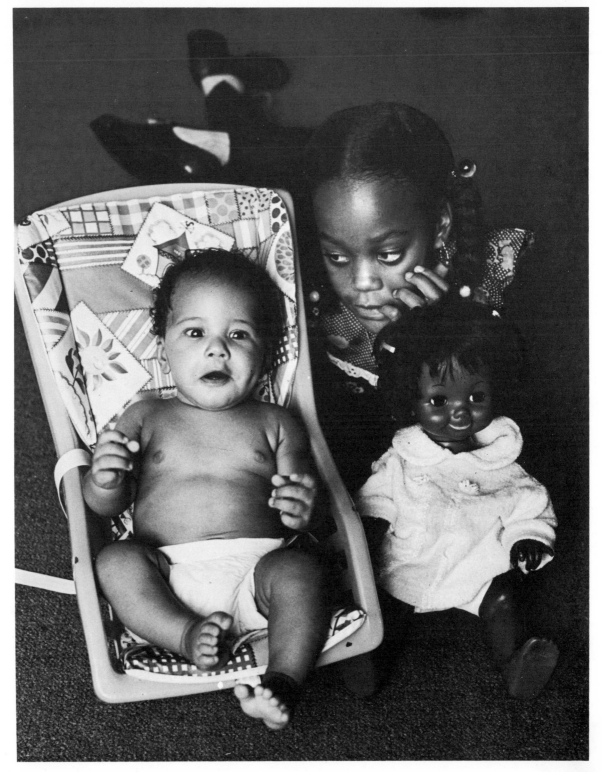

Parents can't expect that everything they do to help their child along will work out like they thought it would. They can expect that what they do, and what they give will be used by their child as tools to express feelings in ways that he can live with. So much for a doll that doesn't grow. It has served its purpose—it is easier for Melissa to be mad at the doll she only loved a little than at the Daddy and Mommy she loves so much.

Melissa knocks her doll off the chair. That doll just makes her angry.

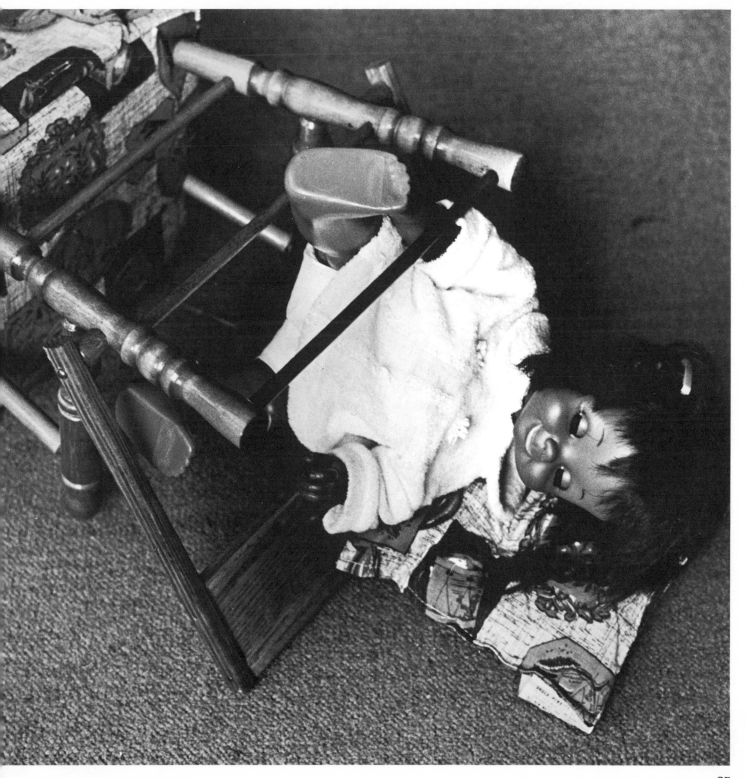

A child changes fast in his first few years—takes himself to the toilet, talks in sentences, makes friends. Sometimes he has to slow down a while, take time to get used to the new step he has taken, get to know his new self, make sure it works.

A new baby in a child's life may make him pause in his growth too. If he was about to take a new step, he may put it off until he is more sure of things. If he has just taken one, he may want to temporarily abandon it, to go back to where he was. If he is just getting used to something new about himself, it may take him longer.

This is not a time to pressure a child. It is a time to like just where and what he is. It is a time to realize that though he is much older than a baby, he is much younger than a grownup. What he is pleased with about himself is plenty for you to be pleased with too.

These are the real things
Charles and Melissa can do

Jump rope. Tie shoes. Eat hotdogs.
Draw pictures. Climb high places.

It is really true. A mother can't do everything for everybody at once. She can't feed a baby and tie a shoelace. She can't bathe a baby and stop a fist fight. She can't rock a baby to sleep and serve popsicles. Any mother feels torn, sometimes mad, sometimes on the verge of tears. This book may help you to explain what babies need, what your child needed and got when he was a baby.

Maybe you have snapshots of that time, so your child can see that he too was fed and held and bathed, just like the new baby.

These are the real things a baby needs: Cuddling and playing naps and baths and food.

And now he has other things he needs. When your child was a baby, he needed his bottle—now he needs cookies and hamburgers, and that is what you give him. When he was little, he needed to be bathed—now he needs to play at the sink, and to shoot water pistols, and that is what you let him do. When he was a baby, he needed to be rocked—now he needs to be hugged, to ride his daddy's shoulders; now he needs a bedtime story; now he needs a little time, after the baby is asleep, to talk with his mommy and daddy, and that is what you do for him.

Sometimes it feels good to make a list—in writing or in pictures—of what a child needed as a baby and what he needs now. Sometimes it feels good to try things he used to do when he was little—and find out they are not really so much fun anymore.

Charles and Melissa need things too.

Jealousy isn't all bad. Squabbling helps a child form ideas of justice: "That's not fair," is a concept as well as an accusation. Teasing helps a child see himself from another's eyes: "Crybaby" is a viewpoint as well as an insult. Sibling rivalry may be a pain in the neck, but it is not an illness. And parents find if they do not always intervene, that children will find ways to work things out together. They will dislike each other; they will like each other too.

Charles and Melissa are finding out something they can do very well is something the baby likes very much. They sure can make noise; Darrell sure likes the racket. They can make him smile. A mother would never have thought of a baby parade.

One day
the children make
a baby parade.
Darrell watches.
He stops crying.
He is interested.
Mommy
is so surprised!

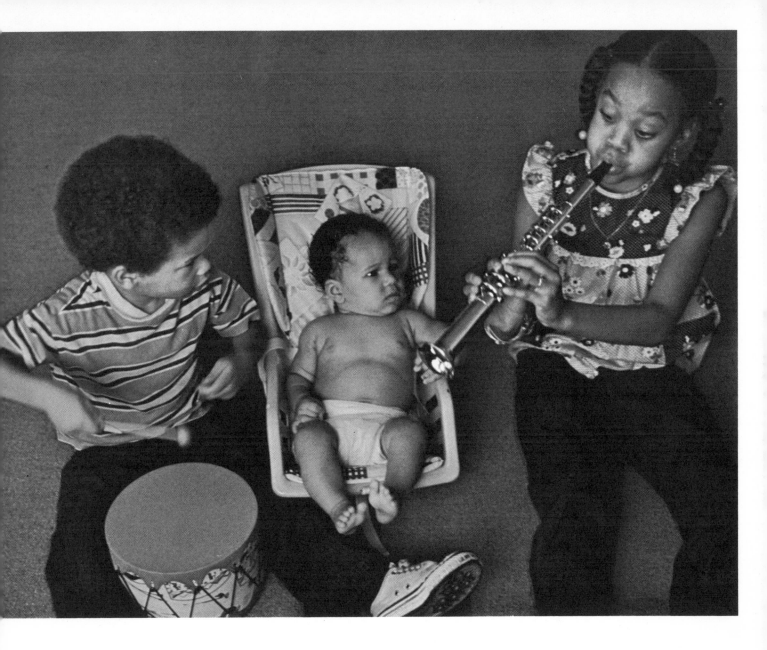

Sooner or later a child asks: "Who do you love the most?" It is honest to tell your child that is a question no mother, no father, can answer. Mommies and daddies don't love one child more than another. They love each the most in a different way. They notice what each child is like; they help him grow into the kind of person he is best at. And that is what they love.

When a child likes himself, he can afford to like others. When he is encouraged to grow in his own way, he can let others grow in theirs. When he is sure of his be-ginnings, he can let another have a beginning too. And when he is sure there is room for him in his family, he will make room for that new baby.

She has time now for Melissa and Charles.
She has room in her lap now.
She has plenty of love for everyone.

And there is room in the family
for that new baby too.